The Printing Press

Chapter 5
**Lesson 84: Digraphs with Plural Endings and
Multi-Syllabic Words with Digraphs**
Lexile® Measure: 570L

ISBN 978-1-62382-040-4

In today's world, it is common to see people reading books. People read books while tanning on beaches. They read on park benches. People read books at bus stops.

During the Middle Ages, finding a book to read was not as easy. Most books back then were written by hand. They were written on parchment. They were very expensive. It took a long time to produce a book written by hand. That is why there were very few books to read.

Only people who had a lot of riches could afford to purchase books — that is, until Johann Gutenberg invented something new. His invention changed the history of the world.

Johann was born in Germany in 1400. His exact birthday is not known. His father was a goldsmith. His family had plenty of riches. They purchased books to use while teaching Johann to read. One of Johann's wishes was to invent a way to print bunches of copies of the same book. That way, many people could read them.

He worked for thirty years to invent a faster way to print books. Many problems came his way. But nothing stopped him from working to make his wish come true.

In 1455, 200 copies of the Bible were printed on Johann's printing press. These copies were printed faster than ever before.

He also invented a new type of ink. It was made with oil. The new ink did not leave splashes on the pages.

These batches of the printed Bible were cheaper than other books. Churches could afford to purchase many copies.

A young man named Christopher read a book that was printed on Johann's printing press. It was about the travels of Marco Polo. The book inspired him to explore the world. It provided him with useful information for his travels. In 1492, he discovered America.

What do you think would have happened if Christopher Columbus had not read that book?

Thanks to Johann Gutenberg, you can read as many books as you want.

Who knows? Maybe you'll read a book that will inspire YOU to invent something. Maybe YOUR invention will change the world.

The End

Comprehension Questions

1. This passage is about which invention?
    a. the sword
    b. the computer
    c. the printing press

2. Johann Gutenberg was born in
    a. a car.
    b. America.
    c. Germany.

3. What could *inspire* someone to play baseball?
    a. listening to flute music
    b. reading a book about cooking
    c. watching a favorite baseball team win a
       big game

4. True or false: Libraries nowadays have more books than libraries in the Middle Ages had.

    a. True

    b. False

5. If you had one dollar, which of the following would you most likely be able to *afford*?

    a. a pencil

    b. a brand-new car

    c. a brand-new backpack

Skill Words

batches	cheaper	parchment	teaching
beaches	churches	purchase	thirty
benches	goldsmith	purchased	wishes
birthday	knows*	riches	written
bunches	nothing	something*	
changed	other*	splashes	

Most Common Words

a	had	one	was
about	hand	only	way
also	have	other*	were
America	he	people	what
as	him	read	while
at	his	same	who
back	if	see	why
before	in	something*	will
but	is	than	with
by	it	thanks	worked
came	knows*	that	working
can	long	the	world
change	made	them	would
come	make	then	years
could	man	there	you
did	many	these	your
do	most	they	
father	named	think	
few	new	time	
find	not	to	
finding	of	use	
for	oil	very	
from	on	want	

Challenge Words

book	discovered	invention	travels
books	ever	Johann	young
born	family	problem	
Christopher	history	took	
copies	information	read	

*both Skill Word and Most Common Word